DPJC9 (22)   80p

THE SMITH INSTITUTE

KU-549-314

New Scotland
New Britain

By Gordon Brown and
Douglas Alexander

Published by The Smith Institute

ISBN 1 902488 03 2

Introduction

When Scotland's first Parliament for three hundred years is elected, a long standing grievance - Scotland's democratic deficit - will finally be eliminated.

For the first time for 300 years Scotland's distinctive institutions will be accountable directly to its people.

New policies for education, health, transport, the environment and for key aspects of economic development can and will be formulated where they should be - in Scotland, by people elected in Scotland.

And now that a Scottish Parliament has been achieved, it can no longer be seriously argued that Scotland's culture, its distinctive institutions or its nationhood are any longer at risk, or that the Government that ensured the Parliament is insensitive to the needs of Scotland.

Indeed, the debate about the future of Scotland in the 90's is now quite different from the 80's. The choice in Scotland - as it is now in Wales - is between Devolution in a new Britain set against a wholly separate State.

And the issue is whether there is any case for moving from home rule to the break up of Britain. Indeed the SNP want a majority in the Parliament to begin what they call "independence negotiations".

This pamphlet argues that the way forward is not a separate Scotland, but a new Scotland in the new Britain.

In 1941 the Clydside socialist James Maxton wrote of the SNP: "They came to us who were international socialists and asked us to give up our internationalism in favour of nationalism. That I was not prepared to do."

And so it is today. Our aim should be not just to build a better country, but to build a better world and to recognise that, in the age of economic interdependence, to build a better country we need to build a better world.

So standing up for Scotland does not mean we need break up Britain. Indeed in today's interdependent economy we are better off together, weaker and worse off apart.

Rivals Scotland and England may sometimes be, but by geography we are also neighbours. By history, allies. By economics, partners. And by fate and fortune, comrades, friends and family. We remain part of a community of shared values.

We are better off with stability under new Labour. We are worse off with new barriers to economic and political stability under the SNP.

We are better off with the new deal for jobs under new Labour, worse off with jobs at risk from separatism under the SNP.

We are better off with £28 Billion invested in the NHS and schools under new Labour, worse off with the SNP building consulates before clinics or classrooms.

And we are better off together, recognising that no citizen of Britain should be a foreigner in Britain: that the SNP policy on citizenship would separate families into "citizens" and "foreigners".

In this pamphlet, as long time supporters of a Scottish Parliament, we show why Devolution - not separation - has been the main historical demand of Scotland.

We show why in a global age of economic interdependence co-operation rather than economic separation makes sense.

And we show how Scotland is leading the democratic renewal of Britain as a multicultural, multiethnic and multinational country.

We show how SNP economics are based on a series of manufactured grievances to which the SNP have been unable to respond.

And we show why Scotland is better off and stronger in Britain, worse off and weaker apart.

Chapter 1

The demand for home rule - Addressing the real grievance

In 1987 in a keynote lecture at the SNP conference William McIllvanney asserted that under Mrs Thatcher, Scotland's sense of identity was under threat as never before.

"We have had bad Governments in the past. We have had Governments whose awareness of Scotland's problems seemed on a par with their knowledge of the other side of the moon. But we have never, in my lifetime, until now, had a Government whose basic principles were so utterly against the most essential traditions and aspirations of Scottish life.

"We have never, until now, had a Government so determined to unpick the very fabric of Scottish life and make it over into something quite different. We have never had a Government so glibly convinced of its own rightness that it demands that one of the oldest nations in Europe should give itself a shake and change utterly its sense of self.

"If we allow her [Mrs Thatcher] to continue she will remove from the word Scottish any meaning other than the geographical.

"We are now so threatened by a Government implacably hostile to the ideas that have nourished Scotland's deepest sense of itself that we must protect ourselves. We will either defend our identity or lose it - there is no other choice."

McIllvanney, as so often, reflected the mood of the times. In the 1980s's, important Scottish civic values - those of community and of social justice - were under attack. The autonomy of Scotland's own civic institutions, from our schools and universities to our health service appeared at risk.

The old settlement between Scotland and the rest of Britain had been able to survive British Government after British Government, even when such Governments were ignorant of, or indifferent to, Scottish traditions.

It could not endure when a British Government set about what Scottish people saw as a systematic undermining of basic Scottish institutions.

And what, in particular, Scotland resented was Scottish institutions and their values being attacked in the name of a British Government claiming for itself the right to be the sole bearer of national identify.

Nowhere in a political context was this threat more obvious than in the imposition of the Poll Tax. No event better typified the cultural threat Scotland perceived than when in 1988, in her Sermon on the Mound, Mrs Thatcher sought to shout down centuries of social action by all the churches in Scotland with her speech to the General Assembly of the Church of Scotland. Narrowly focussed on proving that the parable of the Good Samaritan was about the virtues of wealth creation, she appeared to tell Scottish churches that for hundreds of years they had been wrong and she was right. No example better illustrates how, as McIllvanney had written the year previously "...she takes the axe of her own simplicity to the complexities of Scottish life".

So it was hardly surprising that during the 1980's many Scots came to identify Britishness with Mrs Thatcher's version of it - as the sanctification of self interest, distrust of foreigners and constitutional rigidity. And what they found unacceptable about Thatcherite Britain was not its commitment to enterprise - that would indeed have been strange from the country of James Watt and Andrew Carnegie - but its lack of commitment to social justice.

So with the creation of the Constitutional Convention, Scottish civic society - the very civil society that was under threat: churches, civic leaders, health, education and public services - united and mobilised to create a Scottish Parliament designed to preserve and promote Scottish civic life.

What was required, they agreed, was not just a change in Government, but a change in the way we were governed.

And during this time, there was, from the outer isles to the inner cities, an unquestionable growth of support for a Scottish Parliament to 80 per cent of all the Scottish people.

Indeed, this growing assertiveness in Scotland was a movement that transcended politics: Scottish culture thrived over these last 20 years. Yet the defining quality of this reassertion of distinctively Scottish cultural voices - through pop music to literature - was not a narrow anti-Englishness, but a pride in what was distinctively Scottish.

Hugh MacDiarmid may have described his hobby in Who's Who as "anglophobia", but he was the exception rather than the rule in a cultural tradition this century that ranged from the Glasgow School to the new Scottish writers.

Perhaps it is for this reason, that (as the earlier writings of Stephen Maxwell confirm), modern Scottish Nationalism has not been characterised by the strength of its cultural roots, but has instead sought to position itself as a party defined by a narrower, predominantly economic, appeal.

Of course, before the 1980s the movement for Devolution within Scotland had been strong and the case pressing. Those of us who had consistently supported Devolution had always believed that the absence of democracy in Scotland diminished Scottish civic life. We have campaigned for a Scottish Parliament all our political careers.

But, until Mrs Thatcher, the very existence of Scotland's institutions had never been threatened. Devolution, previously desirable, now became essential.

This is the key to understanding how the hesitant and unenthusiastic majority of the 1979 referendum - before Mrs Thatcher - became the determined and strongly confident majority of 1997. How Devolution became, as John Smith said ... "the settled will of the Scottish People".

It is fitting that from 1987, in the coldest of ideological climates, Scottish civic society united and mobilised in the form of the

Constitutional Convention to preserve and promote Scottish civic life. The Convention reflected widespread concern and legitimised protest. It deliberated on outline and in detail, and as the Devolution settlement ultimately made clear, showed the way forward. As George Kerevan has recognised, it was this ..."dense network of civil society through which Scotland has preserved its identity during the 300 years without a Parliament".

But it was a coalition that the SNP never joined. For what united the Constitutional Convention was a desire to preserve all that was good in what is Scottish. But in its support for what is Scottish, it did not seek to destroy what was British that was of benefit to Scotland. It was for Scottish democracy, not against British democracy.

Its case was to preserve and to advance Scottish institutions and values. What Scots sought to build was a new ethic of community, not a politics of separation. Indeed as Joyce Macmillan has written, what bound Scots together then was a set of values held also by many people in England, and elsewhere too.

The Scottish Parliament established under Donald Dewar's leadership, achieves three radical changes and is, in our view, the modern democratic means of answering the basic question - what best advances Scotland's needs.

First, it ensures the right of representatives directly elected by the Scottish people to make our civic institutions - from education and health, to law and local government - work in the interests of peoples' values. The institutions that have traditionally borne Scottish identity will now reflect Scottish values. The 1990s settlement is an advance on the 1970s in a number of critical respects.

Responsibility for the Universities, for example, excluded in the 1978 legislation, is now devolved to the Scottish Parliament. And the opportunities for reform and modernisation are great indeed. In the age of lifelong learning Scottish education can become once again a world leader. By tackling health inequalities, Scotland can move from merely curative health to a new emphasis on preventive health. Land reform can help us lead the way in environmental care. And we have a chance to tackle the economic and employment causes of our run down council estates.

And no Parliament can have a better start. In total £28 Billion, the largest ever sum allocated to health and education, is available to finance investment in reform over the coming 3 years. It is the equivalent of £14,000 for every Scottish household.

Second, not least because the Parliament is now accepted by all political parties, the permanence of Scottish civic institutions - and indeed the new Parliament - is secured. The capacity of these institutions to reflect Scottish values is safeguarded.

The constitutional consequences of Mrs Thatcher - unintended by her though they were - are that in Scotland at least, another Mrs Thatcher can never again represent the same threat. No second Mrs Thatcher could ever inflict such damage on Scottish civic life again.

There is to the Devolutionary settlement a third dimension that looks far into the future. Scotland is increasingly part of a truly global economy, where decisions, affecting Scottish employees are made at local national and international levels, at all of which Scottish peoples' interests must be recognised.

So, the Devolution plan rightly places in the hands of the Scottish Parliament those key drivers of supply side policy - training and education, business and regional development, Scottish enterprise itself - that are so fundamental to jobs, and future economic success.

This is critical to a country like Scotland where by linking education, technology and the encouragement of new business we have the chance to lead in the knowledge economy of the future.

Indeed many believe we can meet the challenge of the New Information Age by creating a world class environment for information technology firms, by encouraging everything from electronic government and tele-medicine, to R&D clusters and smarter schools.

In all the areas of the new economy, a Scottish Parliament can make a difference, while still benefiting from remaining an integral part of the British economy.

So the new Parliament addresses both the wrongs of the past and the challenges of the future. It is therefore a serious mistake to portray it as some sort of half way house, a mid-point between the status quo and separatism. Nor is it the least autonomy that the British State could get away with.

The Scottish Parliament has been devised as, and is, a modern means of expressing Scotland's relationship with Britain. And it stands on its own.

Indeed the legislation for the Parliament's powers set out to advance the well-being of Scottish people, not in the sheltered economies which gave rise to the old nation states of the past, but in the new global economy with its multilayered institutions.

Devolution shaped to modern needs is not therefore some alien implant into Scottish politics, and it is quite wrong to see it in that way.

The democratic forces that gained strength during the 1980's and brought about this new settlement in the 1990's represented a long tradition of support for Devolution, or, as it was often called, Home Rule. Indeed, historically the demand for Devolution or Home Rule in Scotland has been far stronger, far more persistent, far more deep-rooted than the demand for separatism.

Since the 1880s, with the creation of the Scottish Secretary, the idea of administrative Devolution started in Scotland and calls grew for political accountability in Scotland.

Even a brief survey of the Home Rule movement demonstrates that Home Rule for Scotland has, for most of the century, been and been seen as an alternative to separation, and worthwhile in itself.

When the 1906-14 Liberal Government became the first to support "Home Rule all round", this involved Devolution of power, not the separation of Scotland from the rest of the UK. And when in 1918 a Speakers Conference recommended the creation of Councils for Scotland and other parts of the UK but could not agree who should be in the devolved Councils - existing MP's, nominated or elected representatives - they were thinking of Devolution inside the United Kingdom not separation from it.

When the Scottish Home Rule Association held its first annual meeting in September 1919, the demand was for constitutional reform within the United Kingdom. Its resolution stated: "That this meeting representing all shades of political opinion and industrial activity, being convinced that the present centralised system of Government from London is inefficient and inconsistent with national sentiment, resolves to form itself into a Committee for the purpose of organising and focussing the Scottish demand for self government in respect of Scottish affairs."

So the distinction was clear from the start. The aim was Scottish self government for Scottish affairs to tackle the centralisation of the UK.

The Labour Party National Conference of 1918 added its voice, supporting..."constituted separate legislative assemblies of Scotland, Wales and England, with autonomous administration in matters of local concerns". The powers envisaged were subject to a Westminster constitutional veto: "The Scottish Parliament shall have powers to deal with any Scottish matters except such as determine the concern of and equipment of the Army, Navy, Civil, Diplomatic, Dominion, Colonial, and other Imperial Services." There was a constitutional veto and three categories of business - retained, common business and then devolved services under the Crown.

Throughout the 1920's Home Rule did not mean Separation, but Devolution within the United Kingdom. A statement at the 1922 election made it clear: statutory legislatures for Scotland, Wales and England as well as Ireland were "part of the larger plan of constitutional reform", but the Devolution was for "matters of exclusive local concern".

A Home Rule Bill, introduced in 1924, was modelled on Devolution as it operates in Northern Ireland. The then Labour Government gave the general principle of the Bill their approval. The Bill retained to the UK Parliament majority services including the Post Office, Customs, Army, Navy, Foreign Affairs and Tax Collection. There was to be the same representation for Scotland in the House of Commons. Scottish Members would abstain from voting on English matters. The Memorandum of the Bill suggested the proposals were ..."an extension of the policy of Devolution within the UK." A joint Exchequer Board was to allocate finances. Indeed, Tom Johnson was explicit in saying he did not want to be accused of separation; he wanted a "federal" solution.

More Bills followed during the 1920's. The 1927 Bill of James Barr was a more radical measure arguing for Dominion status, but his proposal that Scottish Mps no longer sit at Westminster caused reaction.

Introducing the 1927 proposal, Tom Johnson stated that there was: "A desire to have both a Parliament and a share in the administration of Imperial affairs, the joint services, including the army, navy, and air force".

When in 1923 the Scottish Home Rule Association advocated Devolution it argued that Home Rule meant the creation of a National Parliament and a National Executive for Scotland. But the Government of the UK would have reserve matters in their control and There would be conjoint administration in other areas. "Home Rule is simply a variety of Devolution but it has two main characteristics that make it important. First it is thoroughgoing and complete Devolution. Second, it is Devolution to a nation - Home Rule is simply natural, thorough, efficient and harmonious Devolution."

In 1918 the proposals were subject to a "constitutional veto". In 1924 the Buchanan Bill was an extension of Devolution within an Imperial Parliament. The 1927 Bill, left shared powers. In 1929 the Labour Party could talk of its commitment to "federal Devolution"; the commitment was explained as autonomous powers in matters of local concern.

So what happened in the 1980's, affirmed in the constitutional settlement of the 1990's, was that this deep rooted and long standing demand of the Scottish people for Devolution gained an unstoppable impetus.

When the bitter experience of the 1980's revealed that civic institutions, that had once been taken for granted, could be at risk. People in

Scotland voted overwhelmingly for change.

So Devolution and Home Rule have had a life of their own - something that was clear even at the birth of the SNP. The resolution that led to the Scottish National Party's establishment in 1934 stated that "...Scotland should set up jointly with England, machinery to deal with these responsibilities and in particular with such matters as defence, foreign policy, and the creation of a customs union".

Indeed in the 1946 statement of aim and policy of the Scottish National Party, it spoke of: "A particularly intimate relationship with other countries of the British Isles is enjoined by geographical and economic considerations. The creation of joint arrangements for the discussion and settlement of matters of mutual concern would be a measure at once natural and beneficial."

But having struggled since its inception to come to terms with the reality of matters of mutual concern within these islands, and the broad appeal of Devolution, the SNP have now opted for the extremism of the break up of Britain.

Just at the time Labour has delivered Devolution, meeting the mainstream aspirations of Scotland, the SNP has rejected the interdependence of our economies and replaced ideas of shared sovereignty with the rest of Britain with proposals for the breakup of the United Kingdom.

Relations with the rest of Britain are to be managed, not by joint agreement, but by a 'Department of External Relations' which would deal with "the rest of the UK, Europe and the wider world".

At the time of unprecedented interdependence and integration between the two countries, the SNP's solution is not to value that interdependence but to break up Britain and remove any vestige of Britishness from Scottish political arrangements.

In 1997, Scotland resisted - as they have at every previous election - the SNP's invitation to succumb to the separatist position.

Indeed while the Devolution settlement of the 1998 represented the culmination of a century of pressure for home rule, it is significant that the Scottish National Party chose to stand apart from the Constitutional Convention and the consensus in favour of Devolution.

There could be no clearer indication that there are two strands in Scottish history: one, the mainstream view, that seeks to address Scotland's need through Home Rule within the United Kingdom; and a separatist agenda that seeks to look back towards a nineteenth century nation state to establish Scotland's future by breaking with the United Kingdom.

Chapter 2

Meeting the challenge of the future

The Devolution settlement that establishes Scotland's Parliament achieves three radical changes.

For the first time, significant Scottish civic institutions will be accountable to representatives directly elected by the Scottish people. Not only that, and secondly, the permanence of Scottish civic institutions, and indeed the new Parliament, is now secured.

And thirdly, Devolution places in the hands of the Scottish Parliament key drivers of modern economic policy - including employment policy and education - that are so fundamental to jobs and Scotland's future economic success.

While the question of the 1980's was whether Scottish nationhood would be deprived of its civic institutions that had survived uninterrupted since the Union, the Scottish Parliament resolves that issue in Scotland's favour.

Indeed, with the creation of a Scottish Parliament, no longer can it be claimed that Scottish nationhood or its civic institutions are at risk. No longer can it even be claimed that Westminster has been insensitive to Scottish needs. The creation of the Scottish Parliament was the first act of the new Government.

So it is now for the SNP to explain why they want to move from Home Rule to separation, and explain what possible gain there can be from imposing new barriers of separation by abandoning anything and everything that is British.

With Devolution achieved the SNP can no longer argue that separation is necessary in a global economy because Scottish nationhood would otherwise be destroyed. What they have to explain is why it is that breaking up Britain is a better response to the new challenges than working together to gain the benefits of the global economy.

It is a fact that in the last three centuries of Scotland's history, the quiet determination to maintain what is distinctively Scottish has never required the abandonment of everything that is British.

There was no desire in Scotland, nor did it make sense, to reject everything that was British in the age of Empire when Scottish people enjoyed some of the prosperity and prospects for employment that came from the World wide opportunities the Empire brought.

There was no desire either, nor did it make sense, to abandon our connection with, or loyalty to, Britain in the half century of total war. Britain was united by shared suffering - the blitz devastated Clydebank as surely as it did Coventry - and shared purpose. And after the war British identity was cemented further by the common endeavour of thereafter building the Welfare State and in particular the health service. When we talk of the National Health Service in Scotland, National means British.

The question therefore is whether, in a new and different age, in a global marketplace, it now makes sense, or indeed there is a real desire, to break the British connection?

During the period of the last SNP rise and fall, the Labour MP, Professor John Mackintosh, wrote of Scottish people's dual identity - being Scottish and British - and argued that to be both Scottish and retain a sense of being British has been the reality for most Scots, and is entirely uncontradictory. Feelings of Scottishness and Britishness could respectively rise and fall, as Mackintosh asserted, without pride in one requiring the rejection of the other.

That the miner, computer worker or pensioner in Scotland has felt common bonds with their counterpart in England arises from three centuries of cross-fertilisation and interaction - what George Galloway calls "intermarriage, intermingling and immigration".

And of course these sentiments felt by Scottish people have ranged in intensity - from feeling Scottish while asserting a pride in being British - perhaps strongest during the shared sacrifice of the war years - to expressing a fierce loyalty for Scotland and yet continuing to feel part of Britain.

But feelings of Scottishness have never required the eradication of Britishness.

Indeed, Professor Neil McCormick has made an important distinction that illuminates Scottish history between "existential nationalism" and "utilitarian nationalism". The first is a nationalism under which the very existence of national identity demands that there should also be a Nation State. But there is also a utilitarian nationalism: here the question is not "how do the Scottish people establish the structures of a Nation State?" But "how as a people do we advance the well being of all?" The repeated answer has been co-operation rather than separation.

The contemporary question therefore is whether, in a new and different age, in a global marketplace, it now makes sense, or indeed there is a real desire, to break the British connection?

The globalisation we are witnessing has two main economic features - interdependent global capital markets and global sourcing of products. In this new age of economic interdependence, decisions that affect economic prosperity will, of course, be made locally, nationally and internationally, and with this multilayered decision-making we are seeing the growth of multilayered institutions across the world.

Some people call the political response a sharing of economic sovereignty. They argue that the real prize for a country in this interdependent economy is not absolute sovereignty, with its 19th century trappings of an old nation state, but rather to maximise influence at every level.

On the face of it this multilayered identity seems entirely compatible with the kind of Scotland emerging in the age of a global economy. Simply put, people feel loyalty to their local community; they feel Scottish; they feel British, and they feel increasingly part of Europe.

Loyalty to one need not carry the price of denial of any other.

This modern reality is recognised across Europe. As Dominique Moisi, the Deputy Director of the Paris based Institut Francais des Relations Internationales, wrote recently: "In the Europe of tomorrow, one will be, say, Scottish, British and European, or Catalan, Spanish and European. To acknowledge these multiple identities in a global age should be a source of strength, creativity and diversity for Europeans."

Most would accept that the challenge of advancing the well being of the Scottish people is best answered by sustaining the institutions and policies that reflect both our identities and these diverse locations on power. Against this backdrop, does it make sense for Scotland to impose new barriers and cut itself off from decision-making which affects us at a British level? There are few economies round the world that are more integrated and more interdependent than Scotland and England.

In the 1960's at the time of the first surge of support for the SNP Jim Sillars wrote: "It is common knowledge that the Scottish economy became fully integrated with the rest of the UK during the first industrial revolution. Industrial and financial patterns set at that time have grown so profound that to separate them now would be as difficult as exacting the original acorn from the giant oak."

At the end of that decade, the 1960's, Scottish GDP per head was around 94 per cent of the rest of the UK and Scottish personal disposable income was around 93 per cent of the rest of the UK. There is now such a degree of convergence that Scottish GDP per head is 99 per cent of the rest of the UK and Scottish personal disposable income is 99.5 per cent.

Such is the degree of integration that the majority of Scotland's trade is with the rest of the UK and thousands of jobs in Scottish and British firms depend on this trade. The figures bear this out, sector by sector. We talk a great deal about the effect of Asia on Scotland. Only 7 per cent of Scotland's exports are to Asia, but over 50 per cent of Scotland's exports are to the rest of the UK.

In almost every area of significance - food and drink, banking, insurance, chemicals, and metal machinery - the rest of the UK is our biggest customer.

It is estimated that 367,000 jobs depend on exports to the rest of the United Kingdom. It represents almost 100,000 direct jobs in manufacturing and over 100,000 direct jobs in services respectively.

We have examined Scotland's top 50 private sector employers. Only seven of them have a home base outwith the UK. In fact, more than half of Scotland's top 50 private sector employers are registered in the rest of the UK. Thus, at a stroke, more than half of employment in Scotland's top private employers derives from non-Scottish UK-based companies.

What is more, many of the largest Scottish private sector employers not only have substantial English interests but a significant share of their British business comes from the rest of Britain - Scottish and Newcastle, John Menzies, Standard Life and Scottish Amicable, are but a few examples.

So to an extent far greater than the Nationalists would care to admit, Scotland's economic future is bound inextricably with the rest of the UK and any instability in the trading relationships between Scotland and the rest of the UK could have a damaging impact on the Scottish Economy and Scottish jobs.

Faced with these facts, the question the Nationalists must answer is why they want to impose on these companies and their employees new barriers arising from separation between Scotland and the rest of the United Kingdom with all the costs and disruption entailed.

No one knows the full extent of the financial costs of imposing a separate market, far less the possible costs in lost business, trade interaction and jobs. When examining economic unions in Europe, the Ceccini report estimated the gains of a single market at between 2.5 - 6.5% of GDP. As surely as Ceccini identified the benefits of barriers coming down, the SNP have consistently refused to acknowledge the additional uncertainties and costs created by imposing new barriers.

What is clear is that whatever happened afterwards there would be very significant costs in setting up financial transactions based on a different currency, in-house transactions in the corporate sector and international banking transfers. Procedures for submitting accounts, regulations, and paying taxes would all have to be costed.

Yet, when asked during the last Parliament about changing currencies at the border, Alex Salmond responded merely that "...these matters are of minor inconvenience."

So if the issue is what best advances the well being of the Scottish people, the case for a British political connection in the age of the global economy is actually even stronger than in the age of Empire.

We would suggest that the real reason why separation has been put on the agenda is not because it is a forward looking approach to the challenges of the global economy but because it offers a superficially easy - but wrong - retreat from global forces of change. Changes in the global economy have not merely created greater integration - common brands, common media, communications and culture - but also, in various places it has led people to seek refuge from these forces.

As the American historian Schlesinger writes of this development: "The more people feel themselves adrift in a vast impersonal, anonymous sea, the more desperately they swim towards any familiar, intelligible protective life raft; the more they crave the politics of identity."

If in the nineteenth century political nationalism arose in face of the uneven development of capitalism, late twentieth century Scottish Nationalism can now be seen as a misguided retreat from and response to modern forces of change.

And it is our view that the SNP have misunderstood not only recent Scottish history but also the real global challenges Scotland must meet in the future.

Their policy is now "independence in Europe". They have conceded that they require to share sovereignty in common decision-making institutions with the rest of Europe, yet they are unwilling to accept the consequences of that insight.

So the contradiction at the heart of SNP's approach is that the SNP now accept the logic of economic interdependence in a global economy and indeed the idea of shared sovereignty. They are prepared to accept it with one glaring exception - when it comes to their relationship with the rest of Britain.

Instead they demand that Scotland's relations with Britain be regulated not by shared decision-making at a British level but by what they call a "Department of External Relations", thus immediately classifying the rest of Britain as a foreign country. This Department of External Relations is to be responsible for "Relations with England, the rest of the UK, Europe and the wider World".

For us, it is a point of principle that whether they are from old communities or new, no citizen of Britain should ever be a foreigner in Britain.

The progressive response to globalisation is not to look inwards, to cut ourselves off, or to retreat to a new form of tribalism in the face of profound change. As Eric Hobsbawm has written, the political project for the left has and should be "for all human beings...", whereas "identity groups" are about themselves, for themselves and nobody else.

So to work for the common good, in a country that has not retreated behind new barriers, but is outward-looking and internationalist, is not merely an expression of a mature patriotism. It is the surest means of ensuring that rather than retreating into the politics of the nineteenth century, Scotland now rises to the economic challenges of the twenty first century.

Chapter 3

The case for the New Britain

In the small print of the Scottish Parliament Election Document of the SNP is a stark statement. A simple majority, 65 seats, next May would be "a mandate for independence negotiations", negotiations they would begin immediately.

So over the next six months the future of Scotland will be decided. For the Nationalists the first priority is separation. Instead, Labour will campaign on health, education and jobs, for a new Scotland in a new Britain, arguing against separation.

Schlesinger has written: "Countries break up when they fail to give ethnically diverse peoples compelling reasons to see themselves as part of the same Nation".

Today the Scottish Nationalists argue that the break up of Britain is inevitable. They claim that what now divides Britain - the distinctive and separate identities of different nations - is greater than what can ever unite it again. The case in 1999 for the Union of 1707, they say, can no longer be sustained.

Of course, there is an old, familiar and widely propagated case for the Union. It was a case first developed with the Union of the Crowns, a case honed to perfection in the age of Walter Scott, one handed down from generation to generation.

Unionism may - as the perceptive historian Linda Colley has argued - have originated in anti-Catholicism, anti-French feelings and the ambitions of Empire. But for two centuries at least Unionism was expressed in support for and deference to traditional British institutions from the Monarchy downwards.

Most recently as Tom Nairn correctly diagnosed, those traditional unreformed institutions have ceased to command the loyalty they once did and ceased to be a sufficiently powerful adhesive force binding Britain together and giving Scottish, Welsh and English peoples common purpose for the future.

Indeed for Nairn the unreformed - and unreformable - Britain is the central reason for supporting a Scottish breakaway. For him the key to the Nationalist renaissance lies not so much in ethnic and linguistic factors ... "but in the slow foundering of the British State", whose central institutions have proved incapable of radical reform. In other words, for Tom Nairn, the strongest argument for a Scottish State is neither the strength of a Scottish culture not the threat to Scottish identity but the failure of the British State. Ironically the British institutions that were once the vehicle for binding Scotland to Britain are now the very argument for separation.

Of course an old Unionism based only on a deferential attitude to ancient institutions is inadequate to meet the challenges of the new world. That is why the most fundamental constitutional changes are being made not only in Scotland, but in Wales, Northern Ireland and in Freedom of Information, the House of Lords and Local Government.

Of course, Nationalists call forth a different fate for our islands, divided into separate national states taught to cherish their separateness, but, in our view, the alternative vision is far stronger: a common purpose, derived from shared values that makes Scotland stronger with Britain, and Britain stronger with Scotland.

That is not a new insight. In the 19th century John Stuart Mill observed that the two elements that defined a nation, were the desire on the part of the inhabitants to be governed together and the "common sympathy" instilled by shared history, values and language.

"Free institutions" he wrote "are next to impossible in a country made up of different nationalities. Among a people without fellow feeling especially if they read and speak different languages, the united public opinion, necessary to the working of representative government, cannot exist."

Of course, the Britain we are talking about is not one forced together by the imposition of a narrow and crude uniformity. It is instead one which celebrates unity from diversity, a multinational Britain in which we gain strength from the interaction of different cultures, the loss of which would diminish us.

And what Mario Cuomo has written of America is true of Britain today. Our vision is of a multicultural Britain in which we gain strength from the interaction of different cultures. Mario Cuomo has written of America: "Most can understand both the need to recognise and encourage an enriched diversity as well as the need to ensure that such a broadened multicultural perspective leads to unity... and not a destructive factionalism that would tear us apart".

Our opportunity is to forge probably the first successful multicultural multiethnic and multinational country. So let us examine the values and then the common endeavours that bind us together.

In 1603 it may just have been a joint Monarch, and in 1707 a common Parliament and little else. Today it is not simply that we share a common island, and a common language, but that we also share a commitment to openness and internationalism, to public service and to justice, to creativity and inventiveness, to democracy and tolerance.

And the British expression of these values today goes far beyond common security and defence and an integrated economy.

The National Health Service was not a specifically Scottish creation. Indeed, it was created by a Welshman, but it serves the whole of Britain.

Of course, we can have a separate NHS in Scotland - indeed it is already administratively devolved - but the ideal that inspires and motivates the staff and the patients of the NHS is that any citizen of Britain has an equal right to treatment irrespective of wealth or race and, indeed, can secure treatment free of charge in any part of Britain.

So when we talk of the National Health Service, national means Britain. As a result of what Professor Richard Titmus once called the "gift relationship" it must not be forgotten that blood freely given by a citizen in any part of Britain is available to any British citizen irrespective of where they stay in Britain.

And it is because we pool and share our resources and because we believe that if the strong help the weak it makes us all stronger, that we all gain from these services and would be diminished by their loss.

The same principle can be seen in both our system of National Insurance and in the allocation of Public Expenditure.

In other countries, citizenship carries understandings about rights and responsibilities, but not exactly the same rights, and the same obligations. And so, although social insurance is a concept that is more admired in theory than today practised in reality, British citizenship is indeed reinforced by the powerful and widely held idea that, as citizens of Britain, we all contribute to the pensions and social protection against sickness, disability and widowhood of each other. And it is the very sharing of risks over 58 million people that maximises the rights of citizenship.

British National Insurance is a sharing of risks by all of us that provide rights for each of us, guaranteeing provision for any insured family or citizen in any part of Britain. Of course, the British idea of national insurance has changed over time and will continue to change. But no one can deny that the sharing of risks among 58 million citizens is a more potent support for the poor and thus for social justice than the sharing of risks among 5 million.

Equally, at a British level, public expenditure is allocated according to need. The Barnett formula is a population-based formula to allocate changes in public expenditure between the countries of the United Kingdom, but the starting point is that resources are allocated on the basis of need.

While, as one academic has written, "The extent of the higher needs has never been established with precision because precision in needs assessment models is impossible", it is however the case that public spending allocation is based on studies like that of 1979 which showed that because of higher morbidity, sparser population, and higher degrees of poverty, Scotland's needs were 16 per cent more per head than England, Wales 9 per cent more, and Northern Ireland 31 per cent more. So the sum is greater than its parts. We gain from our interdependence and would be diminished without it.

So this is a clear dividing line between separatism and those who defend Britain: the pooling of resources to benefit those most in need not to benefit just those of one particular national identity. Public spending allocated according to need, not simply on the assertion of national identity. Taxation according to ability to pay, not national claims. Social justice, not narrow politics of identify the aim.

Yet for the Nationalists, issues of social justice have always been, and must always be, secondary to issues of national identity. For left of centre parties, indeed for most concerned people, social justice comes first. So whereas for Labour, allocation of resources would be on the basis of need (which incidentally benefits Scotland), the SNP would inevitably argue the needs of a millionaire in Scotland before a poor pensioner in England.

Any SNP Government would spend money putting in place the trappings of a Nation State, rather than allocating resources in a manner that advanced social justice. Spending on the costly apparatus of a new National Government would come first. Spending on the National Health Service would be bound to come second. Spending on the Scottish Embassies and Consulates would come before spending on Scottish schools. The logic of nationalism is that the politics of national identity come before the politics of social justice.

We start from a different approach. Our view, that no citizen of Britain should be a foreigner in Britain, is quite distinct from the Scottish Nationalist view of Britain, and the SNP's proposal for a "Department of External Relations".

The Nationalists view of Scottish citizenship has been narrowed in recent years. In 1993 Alex Salmond stated that as well as all those resident in Scotland at the time of independence, "all those who were born in Scotland or who had a parent or grandparent born in Scotland, but are temporarily out of the country, will also be entitled to full membership".

Now the SNP's recent "Parliament and Constitution of an Independent Scotland" document states citizenship will be granted to "all those resident in Scotland on the date of independence and to those who were born in Scotland but are resident elsewhere."

Both of the authors of this pamphlet have family members who would thus be denied Scottish citizenship. Children of Scots, but made foreigners in Scotland. It is now clear that the SNP's rules would divide families all across Scotland into two categories - citizens and foreigners.

Indeed, this new restriction by the SNP on its definition of Scottish citizenship means their right of citizenship is more limited than the criteria for representing Scotland in either football or rugby. For both the SFA and the SRU the entitlement to represent Scotland is established if a parent or a grandparent was born in Scotland.

So the case for a new Scotland being represented in the new Britain is, in the end, quite straightforward - that we gain from common services and are diminished without them; that we achieve more working together than working apart; that unity, out of diversity, gives us strength; that solidarity, the shared endeavour of working and co-operating together, not separation, is the idea of the future and the idealism worth celebrating.

We, of course, are talking not just about what Britain is, but what Britain can be. A new Britain where the Constitution reflects a new relationship between individual community and the State.

Of course, much remains to be done. But we have already seen the establishment of Scottish, Welsh and Northern Ireland Democracies, and a Bill of Rights. We are in the middle of the reform of the House of Lords. And we will shortly see a Freedom of Information Bill and plans for bringing local government closer to the people. These are not simply protections for the individual against the State. These are measures that attempt to forge a new relationship in which the individual is enhanced by membership of their community, and the State enables and empowers rather than controls or directs.

So the challenge of representing the interests of Scottish people should not require us to define ourselves on the basis of our borders, but to define ourselves - as McIllvanney argued a decade ago - on the basis of our values. And a new Scotland represented in this new multinational multicultural Britain means a new politics of diversity and solidarity, rather than the old politics of division and separation; a Scotland reborn, not a Scotland apart.

Can Britain become, as we would like, the first successful multicultural multiethnic multinational country?

America is, of course, already a multicultural multiethnic state. As Trevor Philips has written: "Americans have had to construct an idea of their nation from huge groups of people who had barely heard of each other before landing on American soil". By contrast, Britain ... "has a thousand or more years of nation building behind it, and historically speaking, we have had ripples, rather than waves, of immigration; change has been incremental".

So while America's national identity absorbs and transcends the diverse ethnicities that came to its shores. In Britain our challenge is different: to succeed not just as a multicultural and multiethnic country but as a multinational one as well. It is a Britain of diversity where the common culture is enriched and reshaped by the very act of citizens entering into it.

This form of coming together, rather than separatism, is the way of the future. The challenge is acknowledge and celebrate diversity without breaking the bonds of cohesion, common ideals, common political institutions, common language and common values that holds the country together.

There are Scottish Nationalists who seek to accommodate in their vision a recognition of the merits of multiculturalism, yet they struggle with the consequences of this insight. In a recent article, George Kerevan claimed: "the Scottish melting pot is one of the reasons that the concept of Britain no longer works". The internal incoherence of such a tortured argument exposes the enduring question: if such Nationalists believe diversity can build strength, then why should there be new unnecessary barriers imposed? If they do believe there should be new barriers, let them now defend the need for such barriers, if they cannot agree that the best policy is the new Scottish Parliament.

It remains the case that for both Scotland and England our internationalism is tested on our doorstep - whether being Scottish or English requires us to break up the partnership of the peoples of Britain and eliminate every vestige of decision-making that is British.

In their attitudes to Britain in the 1990's, the SNP threaten to be the mirror image of Mrs Thatcher's attitude to Scotland in the 1980's. If the threat then was a Britain intolerant to much that is Scottish, the risk now is a Scotland intolerant to much that is British. There is no idealism in moving from the narrow nationalism of Mrs Thatcher to that narrow nationalism of the SNP.

The internationalism we will want to celebrate in the 21st century is one that will foster, and by its institutions, sustain greater interaction and cross-fertilisation - and, indeed, solidarity - across cultures, communities and people. Breaking down barriers, instead of imposing new ones. And Britain has a chance of doing so.

This journey to a new Britain calls for a high road of tolerance of diversity. And a mature patriotism based on confidence and security.

The SNP's low road would be a narrow nationalism which is regenerating into the politics of grudge and manufactured grievance.

We prefer the high road which recognises our dependence upon each other and the contribution we can all make to the common good.

Chapter 4

The politics and economics of separation

The long battle for a Scottish Parliament will finally be won when Scotland goes to the polls this year. The new Parliament brings to an end a long standing grievance - the absence of democracy.

But it also changes the terms of the debate in Scottish politics. As long as Devolution was denied the SNP were able to conflate two distinct propositions - the majority wish for Devolution with the minority wish for separatism. Because the case for democracy in Scotland was so strong they argued that its denial made the case for abandoning Britain.

With the advent of a Scottish Parliament, the SNP cannot any longer claim that Scotland is being suppressed or even ignored. But unable to cope with the new politics of making the Parliament work, and unable to defend the costly and unjustifiable barriers that separation would impose on business, on citizens, and on other public services, the SNP have fallen back on the politics of grudge and manufactured grievance.

It is time to expose not only the mythical nature of the claims that they peddle but also highlight the cost of the unnecessary barriers they threaten to impose.

Each claim they make - that Scotland receives less public spending than a per capita allocation entitles it to; that Scotland contributes more tax than its population share; that Scotland has a surplus, not a deficit; that a Scottish currency could be created painlessly; and that interest rates would be lower as a result - is demonstrably wrong.

Scotland, says the SNP, is denied its proper share of Public Spending. This is simply wrong. Spending per person is far more in Scotland than in Britain as a whole. The latest figures for identifiable public expenditure published in the Public Expenditure Statistical Analysis show that Scotland received 24% more than England, per head, in 1996-97. Identifiable government spending in Scotland was about £5,000 per head in 1996-97 compared to almost £4,000 per head in England. The picture does not change dramatically once non-identifiable public expenditure is added in. Defence is the main component of this, accounting for almost two-thirds of non-identifiable expenditure, and the latest publication shows that Scotland's share of both MOD contracts and the location of personnel (both military and civilian) is roughly in line with its population share.

The fact is that in the UK public expenditure is allocated on a principle most people can accept - on the basis of need. The current UK financial system results in Scotland receiving more expenditure from central government because of its needs.

Scotland, we are told, is running a public sector surplus. But the latest government figures for 1995-96 showed Scotland to be running a deficit of around £7.5 Billion. These are figures based on a methodology that all serious outside commentators consider the best available. Projections into the future by the Labour party put this deficit at over £5 Billion a year for each year of the first Scottish Parliament.

At a time when the UK deficit is finally coming under control, Scotland will be exhibiting a sizeable structural deficit in public finance.

Scotland, in the SNP view, could pay its way with its oil revenues. This is not the case. With oil production slowing and oil prices low, the position throughout the nineties has been that Scotland has been running a deficit.

The latest official estimate, assuming 90 per cent of North Sea Oil revenues came to Scotland, is for 1995-96 and shows a deficit of over £5 Billion. Again Labour Party projections are for this figure to average £3.75 Billion a year during the first Scottish Parliament. £3.75 Billion is a huge gap to close. It is over two-thirds of the total NHS budget in Scotland or the equivalent of around 25p on the basic rate of income tax.

The SNP sums on separation do not include any provision for the extra costs involved if Scotland were to extricate itself from the rest of the UK. There is nothing included in the deficit projections above for the additional expenditure needed for covering (and not sharing) the cost of Defence, for Scottish Embassies, Consulates and Trade Missions, for new and expensive Taxation and Social Security Systems or all the other apparatus needed for a modern 21st century State. Just sharing out the UK's assets is not the answer. There are very significant economies of scale which accrue to each of the constituent parts of the UK which would be lost if any one part broke up from the rest. Putting to one side the difficulties of apportioning such assets, less than one-tenth of the UK Embassies would give Scotland less than one-tenth of the current representation abroad. The rest would have to be paid for or foregone. The SNP have consistently failed to make clear what the extra cost would be or what would be lost if this cost was not to be met.

Nowhere is there a greater unwillingness to face up to the costs of separatism than in broadcasting. Despite the fact that the BBC was created by a Scot, the SNP want a wholly separate Broadcasting Corporation.

The present BBC Licence Fee raises around £175 million in Scotland. But funding one wholly Scottish TV channel with the range, quality, and current output of BBC1, together with Radio Scotland, could cost up to £800 Million a year. That alone could quadruple the licence fee, from £97.50 to £400 - and that is before any discussion of a Scottish equivalent to BBC2, and radio stations to match the range of BBC Radio 1, 2, 3, 4 and 5. Because there are economies of scale in servicing 58 million rather than 5 million, Scotland simply could not afford on the present licence fee the level of service the BBC gives now. A 'Scottish Broadcasting Corporation' would have to negotiate to buy in - if it could afford them - everything from high cost dramas and soaps like Eastenders to international news coverage which requires correspondents in all parts of the world. The negotiating edge would rest with the bigger BBC the Nationalists would have abandoned. Instead of having direct influence we would be in danger of being more dependent.

And the story of extra costs for other new institutions is as telling, for everything from Customs and Inland Revenue to high technology defence equipment and central government running costs.

On top of avoiding the questions of how Scottish public finances would be balanced and of how the costs of Separation would be paid for the SNP also tell us that Scotland can afford a 10p Corporation Tax rate. This claim is absurd, and of course, it flies in the face of European Single Market Policy, which the SNP say they support.

The proposal ignores the problem of how to fill the £1.5 Billion shortfall in Government revenues resulting from such a tax cut. The answer of course is that personal taxes would have to rise to compensate. This is exactly what happens in Ireland where the highest personal tax rate comes in at around £13,000 rather than at over £30,000 in Scotland.

The SNP claim that - over time - this tax policy will result in increased tax revenues. They base their assumptions on Ronald Reagan's tax cutting strategy of the early 1980's. The result of Ronald Reagan's tax policies, however, was the biggest ever budget deficit in the history of the USA. They then claim it's based on the so-called Laffer Curve. The idea behind the Laffer curve has been around for over a century but even today nobody could confidently draw its shape; and this shape would no doubt be different depending on whether it was Income Tax, VAT or Corporation Tax that was being studied. In any case Ronald Reagan's policy advisers made no claim that a Laffer curve would work to make their tax cuts wholly self-financing. What evidence there is suggests that, in the longer term, increased revenue does not match lost revenue.

Scotland is worse off, in the SNP's view, because it is denied its own currency. But their argument on this subject has no coherence. They say they want to join the single European currency, but they avoid the issue of how they would meet the criteria set down in The Maastricht Treaty. They also ignore any problems that might occur if Scotland's economy was not in synch with the rest of Europe. They do not analyse this situation as this Government has done, they simply ignore it. When pushed on what would happen between Independence and joining the single European currency, the SNP admit that they would simply peg any Scottish pound to the UK pound. This would result in an interest rate premium having to be paid for a new currency in a small State, and yet it would still rise and fall with the fortunes of the pound. The SNP policy would risk higher interest rates and less currency stability with the markets around the world needing to be convinced of its merits and the monetary policies that underpinned it.

And it would not be long before any such separate Scottish State became aware of this. If the SNP wanted to join the single European currency it would need to meet the Maastricht criteria. One such criterion is that the annual fiscal debt should be no more than 3 per cent of GDP. Even assuming Scotland can claim 90 per cent of North Sea Oil GDP, most of which does not actually accrue to Scots, it would not meet this criterion in the future. This failure is based simply on Scotland's existing fiscal balance: the position would worsen with the costs of separation included, or with Corporation Taxes cut. In such a situation Scotland would be forced to raise taxes or cut services to allow for entry.

In the end each of these manufactured myths reflects a deficit in SNP thinking and their search for electoral slogans. A consistent thread running through the SNP's economic analysis is their refusal to accept any cost associated with Scotland separating itself from Britain.

Perhaps then, business leaders' doubts over the SNP's tax polices are warranted. The promise is for lower business taxes, the harsh reality is a threat of higher taxes all round.

In contrast, with Devolution in place and Scotland's civic institutions preserved and promoted, the needs of the new Scottish economy will be properly addressed at all levels. With the risks and losses from separation becoming clear, the question Scots will now ask is not what is the point of Britain: now that these manufactured grievances have been exposed, the real question is what is the point of the SNP?

Conclusion

The battle between social justice and separatism

When Scotland's new Parliament meets for the first time this year, its 129 Members will already be making history. For the first time in 300 years, Scotland's civic institutions will be directly accountable to the elected representatives of Scotland. But when the 129 Members sit down to debate the future of education, health and social services, they will have an unprecedented and historic opportunity to change the face of Scotland for our generation.

Scottish education in the era of lifelong education can become again a world leader. With a commitment to tackle health inequalities, the NHS can pioneer preventative, as well as curative, medicine. Local Government can be modernised to better meet the needs of Scotland's communities. And, rightly, Devolution places in the hands of the Scottish Parliament those key drivers of supply side economic policy - training and education, transport and infrastructure, and Scottish enterprise itself - that are vital to modern economic success. By linking education, new technology and the encouragement of business development, Scotland has a chance to lead - as the Cadence development shows - in the knowledge economies of the future.

So Scotland's new Parliament will address both the wrongs of the past and the challenges of the future. It is therefore a serious mistake to portray Devolution as a sort of half-way house, as if it were an unstable mid-point between the status quo and separation. With its new powers, the new constitutional settlement between Scotland and Britain is designed to advance the well being of Scotland in the world, far from the sheltered national economies of the past, by embracing the opportunities of the interdependent global economy of the future.

And because of Labour's public spending decisions, the Scottish Parliament will start with unprecedented additional resources to meet these challenges. Over the next three years Scotland will be able to invest more than £28 Billion on education and health, more money than at any time in our history, indeed the biggest increase in health and education investment we have seen. It amounts to £14,000 invested in health and education for every family in Scotland. This will pay for a range of major reforms - a nursery place for all three and four year olds; 5,000 new classroom assistants for our primary and secondary schools; new hospitals; and a new appointment service for GP visits.

By contrast it is in the very logic of Nationalism - central to their commitment to set up a wholly separate State - that the first call on the resources is the cost of setting up the full blown apparatus of a nation State: from a separate currency to Embassies and Consulates overseas.

So the real battle in Scotland in May 1999 will now be between those who put the politics of social justice first, and those who practice the politics of national identity above and before anything else.

There is and always has been more to Scottish politics than identity politics. Solidarity - and working together - offers Scotland more than separation - and splitting ourselves apart. That is why a politics based on the expansive vision of social justice will defeat the narrow divisiveness of Nationalism.